The
LITTLE BOOK OF
GOING GREEN

# The
# LITTLE BOOK OF
# GOING GREEN

*Really* Understand Climate Change, Use Greener Products, Adopt a Tree, Save Water, and Much More!

*Harriet Dyer*

Skyhorse Publishing

Skyhorse Publishing books may be purchased in bulk at special discounts for sales promotion, corporate gifts, fund-raising, or educational purposes. Special editions can also be created to specifications. For details, contact the Special Sales Department, Skyhorse Publishing, 307 West 36th Street, 11th Floor, New York, NY 10018 or info@skyhorsepublishing.com.

Skyhorse® and Skyhorse Publishing® are registered trademarks of Skyhorse Publishing, Inc.®, a Delaware corporation.

Visit our website at www.skyhorsepublishing.com.

10 9 8 7 6 5 4 3 2 1

Library of Congress Cataloging-in-Publication Data is available on file.

Cover design by Qualcom
Cover illustration credit: iStock
Text by Sophie Martin

Print ISBN: 978-1-5107-4173-7
Ebook ISBN: 978-1-5107-4174-4

Printed in China

# *Contents*

**INTRODUCTION**......................................................**7**

**WHAT IS CONTRIBUTING TO CLIMATE CHANGE?**................**11**
    Plastics............................................................12
    Fossil Fuels.......................................................30
    Industrial Agriculture.........................................49
    Deforestation....................................................64
    Human Population.............................................83

**HOW CAN WE REDUCE OUR CARBON FOOTPRINT?**...........**93**
    Businesses.........................................................94
    Individuals........................................................102

**RESOURCES**.......................................................**110**

WE HAVE FORGOTTEN
HOW TO BE GOOD GUESTS,
HOW TO WALK LIGHTLY
ON THE EARTH AS ITS
OTHER CREATURES DO.

BARBARA WARD

# INTRODUCTION

The human impact on global climate change has only relatively recently been realized. Arguably, the father of climate-change science is Svante Arrhenius from Sweden, whose work, published in 1896, opened the channel of thought on the topic of the negative impact fossil fuels might have on the planet. However, it wasn't until greater funding became available in the 1950s that researchers could get firm data in place to start to prove their ideas. Then, in 1988, the United Nations founded the Intergovernmental Panel on Climate Change to assess the relevant studies. Research continues, but it is now clear that human progress has adversely affected our environment.

Up until the middle of the eighteenth century, though coal was also used, the main source of fuel was wood—a renewable biomass energy source. Then the Industrial Revolution arrived and caused a shift in the way humans lived. Coal overtook wood as the primary source of energy and the population of the world exploded, meaning there was a bigger demand for this energy source. From that point, there was no going back; we continued advancing and soon discovered oil and natural gas could also serve as energy sources, which further contributed to climate change. Unaware of the consequences it would have, we pumped toxic chemicals and gases into the atmosphere, creating "the greenhouse effect" (where greenhouse gases act like a blanket trapping heat inside the Earth's atmosphere) and causing an increase in global temperatures we now call "global warming."

Although many of us are aware of the damage caused to the planet by human progress, few of us are actively trying to reduce how much we contribute to it. Consumerism has become a central focus in society: we have come to expect too many things and take too much for granted, whether it's the expectation of foreign travel, owning the newest technological innovation, fast food consumption, commuting to work, or simply flicking the heating on at the first sign of cold. We bury our heads in the sand about the impact we have on the environment and spend little time addressing how we could change our lives for the good of the planet. We can't just hope that other people will take charge of making improvements—every one of us needs to be involved to have an impact.

This book is an introduction to the main ways we are damaging the environment and how we can each contribute to being more earth-friendly.

# WHAT IS CONTRIBUTING TO CLIMATE CHANGE?

# PLASTICS

## WHAT IS PLASTIC?

Plastic as we know it today was invented in 1907 (over a hundred years ago!). From egg timers and phones, to toothbrushes and plumbing pipes, plastic is everywhere. This man-made material is produced from petroleum or natural gas, both of which are non-renewable resources, and both the amount and types of plastic we use are continuing to increase at an alarming rate.

## WHY IS PLASTIC USED SO MUCH?

There are countless reasons why this synthetic material is now an inherent part of our day-to-day lives, including its versatility, durability, imperviousness to water, and ability to withstand heavy weights. It is also a manufacturer's dream, due to low production costs compared with other greener alternatives, such as glass and bioplastics.

## WHAT ARE BIOPLASTICS?

They look, feel, and are almost the same as traditional plastics, but instead of using harmful chemicals, natural chemicals such as corn starch are used in the production process. Compared with non-biodegradable plastics, they are compostable, emit almost 70 percent fewer greenhouse gases when they biodegrade, and use just one-third of the energy needed to create plastic from carbon.

## DO THE PROS OF PLASTIC OUTWEIGH THE CONS?

Although it may be a cheap, flexible, and long-lasting material to manufacture, plastic comes at a significant cost to our planet. Two of the biggest causes for concern are its energy-intensive and non-renewable production and its inability to biodegrade: this in turn affects both the planet's atmosphere, as it is constantly being pumped full of harmful fossil fuels, and its wildlife as we struggle to keep the waste at bay.

# WATER AND AIR, THE TWO ESSENTIAL FLUIDS ON WHICH ALL LIFE DEPENDS, HAVE BECOME GLOBAL GARBAGE CANS.

JACQUES COUSTEAU

## HOW HARMFUL ARE PLASTICS? THE FACTS

→ Around 300 million tons of plastic is produced worldwide each year. Of that, approximately ten percent is recycled.

→ Each year, 17 million barrels of oil are used in the production of America's water bottles alone—that's the equivalent of running more than 1 million cars for a year straight!

→ The great Pacific garbage patch, an area of the ocean which is so highly concentrated in plastic debris that it looks like an island, is estimated to be 2.7 meters deep and twice the size of Texas.

→ Approximately one million sea birds and 100,000 marine mammals die each year because of plastics in our oceans.

→ Harmful plastic chemicals, which can alter hormone balance and contribute to a

> number of negative health effects, are
> absorbed by the human body.
>
> → By 2050, it is estimated that there
> will be more plastic than fish in the
> planet's oceans.

## IS PLASTIC DESTROYING OUR MARINE LIFE?

Yes. The worst-affected species are fish, sea turtles, seabirds, and all sea mammals. The animals either catch infections from plastic wounds, get entangled in plastic waste, or ingest the plastics, which leads to them suffocating and drowning. In 2010, a Californian grey whale was found dead on the shore and post-mortems later found that it had a pair of tracksuit bottoms, a golf ball, more than 20 plastic bags, small towels, duct tape, and surgical gloves in its stomach. Sadly, sick or dead animals washing up on shore with their stomachs lined with plastics are now a common occurrence.

Not only does plastic affect the individual animals that ingest it, it also has a knock-on effect on their young. For example, adult seabirds that feed on the oceans' surfaces are likely to give the plastic to their chicks as food, which leaves them either malnourished or kills them. In one study, researchers found that 98 percent of the chicks tested contained some sort of plastic debris. And even when the animal dies and its body decomposes, the plastic still remains in the ocean.

As the planet's marine life is harmed, we are also inadvertently harming ourselves as we consume fish and ingest the plastics. The "plastic food cycle" is therefore a threat to many areas of life and it is constantly getting worse as we create more and more.

## HOW DOES PLASTIC FIND ITS WAY INTO OUR OCEANS?

Around 80 percent of marine debris comes from the land, including litter left on beaches that is then taken by the sea at high tide, and excess "runoff" waste that has escaped from factories, construction sites, and landfills, and made its way into the water cycle. During periods of heavy rain and winds, trash left on the streets can also reach the oceans as it is forced down drains. Other plastics are dropped or blown into rivers that eventually lead to the sea; then there are the plastic products that are flushed down the toilet, including wipes and cotton buds. Other debris is literally lost at sea when boats and ships capsize and their contents are leaked into the waters. A heavy storm in 1992 caused a shipping vessel containing thousands of plastic rubber ducks to fall overboard and even today people are finding these toys washed up on shores around the world.

## THE PROBLEM WITH NURDLES

Ever heard of nurdles? Shipped around the world, these tiny plastic pellets are used in manufacturing for the production of plastic. Billions and billions are used each year and find themselves washed up on the shore due to the industry's mishandling. The next time you take a stroll along the beach, count how many you spot in one area—you'll be surprised at the numbers. These little pieces of plastic are a huge threat to the oceans as they are eaten by marine animals. Unfortunately, there is no ultimate solution to this wide-spread problem as the billions of pieces that are circulating the oceans will remain there for a long, long time—they do not biodegrade, they will only break up into smaller and smaller pieces ready to be absorbed by marine life. It is the responsibility of the plastics industry to literally clean up its act. The public is also working together and participating around the world in beach clean-ups. In 2015, the National Ocean Service administered a global clean-up where around 680,000 volunteers removed more than 15.5 million pounds of litter from beaches and coastal areas.

## HOW HAVE WE LET PLASTIC
## BECOME SUCH A GLOBAL PROBLEM?

Some countries are better at controling plastic waste than others—for example, the Swedes recycle almost 100 percent of their household waste items. However, that's not to say we couldn't all do a better job of keeping our planet cleaner. In the UK, for example, 38.5 million plastic bottles are thrown away per day. They also account for 40 percent of the litter found in the country. In America, 500 million plastic straws are used every day—if you connected the straws together in a line it would be the equivalent length of two-and-a-half times the circumference of the Earth. Overall, the world has seen a 620 percent increase in the amount of plastic over the past 40 years and not one piece of it is yet to have fully biodegraded.

## HAS OUR LOVE OF PLASTICS GONE TOO FAR?

The figures and facts are shocking and it would be optimistic to say that any of the damage is reversible, especially as our lives are becoming more and more fast-paced and we increasingly favor disposable items because they are more practical. There are ways to reduce the production of new plastics by recycling, yet statistics show that there is a lot of room for improvement: only 9 percent of discarded plastic has been recycled to date. As well as reducing the demand for new plastic to be produced, there are a number of social and environmental benefits to be gained by recycling plastics, including:

→ Saving energy—the recycling process requires only 12 percent of the energy used to create new plastic.

→ Quick turnaround—retailers can see a recycled product back on their shelves within a month.

→ Job creation—helping the environment also increases employment: recycling opens up 6 times more job opportunities than using landfills and 36 times more than incinerating.

## HOW TO IDENTIFY DIFFERENT TYPES OF PLASTIC

A staggering 90 percent of Britons say that they'd recycle more if the process was made easier. When you're rushing around in the morning to get the bins out, knowing which plastics are recyclable and which aren't is half the battle and one of the reasons why we favor the one-stop garbage bin. One way to make sorting plastics a less arduous task is to look inside the well-known recycling symbol (the Mobius loop) for a number from one to seven. This is what they mean:

 PET or PETE (Polyethylene terephthalate)—mainly clear drinks bottles and some food packaging. Recyclable but not reusable.

 HDPE (High-density polyethylene)—bottles used for things like milk, dish liquid, and cosmetics. Recyclable and reusable.

 PVC (Polyvinyl chloride)—clear food wrapping, shower curtains, toys. Difficult to recycle.

 LDPE (Low-density polyethylene)—bags to package bread, grocery bags, squeezable bottles, four-/six-pack can holders. Currently difficult to recycle, although plans are in place to try to change this. A number of supermarkets take grocery bags for recycling.

PP (Polypropylene)—cereal bags, bottle tops, margarine tubs, chip bags, straws. Reusable and occasionally recyclable, e.g. cereal bags and margarine tubs can be recycled.

PS (Polystyrene)—packaging for fragile objects, to-go cups. Not reusable and currently difficult to recycle, although plans are in place to try to change this.

Other—plastics such as acrylic glass, nylon, polycarbonate, and items made of a mixture of plastics. Not reusable and difficult to recycle.

## THINGS TO NOTE ABOUT RECYCLING

Unfortunately, recycling differs between regions, as some facilities are more equipped and advanced than others. Therefore, it's always best to check your local council website to see what they accept.

Again, don't assume that an item displaying the Mobius loop without a number inside can be recycled as this isn't always the case. Instead it represents that an item is *capable* of being recycled but your local recycling center may not take it.

The website www.epa.gov/recycle gives a good overview of the majority of household items we use in the US—from hairdryers and inhalers, to sofas and electronics—with a short description of whether, how, and where the product can be recycled.

WE LIVE IN A DISPOSABLE
SOCIETY. IT'S EASIER
TO THROW THINGS OUT
THAN TO FIX THEM.

NEIL LABUTE

## CAN WE STILL MAKE A DIFFERENCE?

There is a shocking amount of plastic in our oceans and only recently have we realized the consequences it's having for marine life. However, since this discovery, changes have been made and we are increasingly thinking about the future, which has already reduced the amount of plastics being used and thrown away. Here are some of the initiatives that have been put into action around the world:

→ **5p bag fee**—since its introduction, England's plastic bag usage has dropped by 85 percent.

→ **Banning plastic straws**—pub chain Oakman Inns stopped automatically serving straws with drinks and has reduced its use of them by 100,000 per month. Many independent shops in the US have also taken the leap.

→ **Tattooing avocados**—Marks and Spencer has started using laser tattoos instead of labels to display the barcode, best before date, and country of origin. The retailer estimates an annual saving of five tons of glue and ten tons of label and backing paper.

- **Using recycled plastics for packaging**—89 percent of cosmetic retailer Lush's packaging comes from recycled materials. Moreover, its pots and bottles are made with 100 percent post-consumer recycled (PCR) plastic, saving around 65 tons of carbon dioxide (800 barrels of oil) every year.

- **Banning plastic-stemmed cotton swabs**—many retailers have banned the sale of these types of cotton swabs, and in fact, following a campaign by environmental group Fidra, Johnson & Johnson now only produce those with paper stems. According to clean-up studies, over 23 plastic cotton swab sticks are found on every 100-meter stretch of beach in the UK.

# *Fossil* FUELS

## WHAT ARE FOSSIL FUELS?

Fossil fuels include coal, oil, and natural gas and are named so because the fuels were formed millions of years ago from the remains of living organisms. They are non-renewable sources of energy that use oxygen and release environmentally harmful carbon dioxide when burned. We rely on these fuels to run our cars, produce electricity, and operate our power industry and manufacturing. In short, they are indispensable to the way we live now.

## WHY ARE FOSSIL FUELS USED SO MUCH?

Although extraction is relatively expensive, it is a much cheaper source of energy compared with installing wind and solar technologies. Once the fuels have been extracted, they are safe and stable to transport across the world, either via large trucks or in pipes underneath the ground. They are known to be the most economical fuels, as they burn slowly and release more energy as a result, which is why businesses and individuals are so dependent on them. To make sure the energy we need to power our homes and workplaces is constant, governments the world over subsidize the oil firms as an incentive to find and transport more and more of the sources of energy we depend on, which in turn makes the cost cheaper for all parties.

## BUT SURELY THE BENEFITS OF FOSSIL FUELS OUTWEIGH THE DISADVANTAGES?

Although these fuels may be cheap and easy to extract, they are doing a lot of damage to the planet. The main issue is their effect on the world's air pollution. As they are burned, they release excessive amounts of carbon dioxide, as well as other toxic chemicals such as nitrogen dioxide, sulphur dioxide, and carbon monoxide, which trap heat from the sun and force temperatures to rise. Fossil fuels are widely said to be the biggest contributors to climate change, harming the atmosphere and affecting our cardiovascular health. Additionally, they are non-renewable sources of energy, which means they can't be replenished once all the supplies have been used. Based on a study carried out in 2015, it is estimated that coal will run out in 115 years, natural gas in 50 years, and oil in 50 years. At the rate we are using them, alternatives need to be put in place quickly if the world's economic structure and globalization are to be maintained.

# THE SHIFT TO A CLEANER ENERGY ECONOMY WON'T HAPPEN OVERNIGHT, AND IT WILL REQUIRE TOUGH CHOICES ALONG THE WAY. BUT THE DEBATE IS SETTLED. CLIMATE CHANGE IS A FACT.

BARACK OBAMA

## HOW HARMFUL ARE
## FOSSIL FUELS? THE FACTS

→ Extraction of fossil fuels requires an estimated 3 to 6 million gallons of water and 15,000 to 60,000 gallons of chemicals per well. Disconcertingly, many of the chemicals used in the process are undisclosed to regulators—however, one study found that 25 percent of the known chemicals could cause cancer or other mutations, while half could cause severe illnesses and diseases.

→ If offshore drilling goes wrong, it can be devastating. In 2010, an oil rig explosion in the Gulf of Mexico killed 11 workers and released the equivalent of 4.9 million barrels of oil into the ocean.

- → Approximately 400 million tons of excess carbon dioxide–equivalent emissions are generated worldwide each year at oil drilling sites.

- → Surface mining for coal has impacted nearly 1.4 million acres of land in America's Appalachia region, where excess soil and rock are dumped into streams and valleys, preventing water flow and damaging existing ecosystems.

- → Between 1990 and 2000, around 10,000 underground coal miners died of black lung disease worldwide, while a Harvard study found that surface coal miners have an increased risk of contracting severe lung, cardiovascular, and kidney diseases.

> → Burning fossil fuels releases a number of toxic chemicals and contributes directly to global warming and ill health. Each year, an estimated 6.5 million people worldwide die from heart and respiratory conditions linked to air pollution.

## THE EFFECT OF GLOBAL WARMING ON THE WEATHER AND ENVIRONMENT

It's often difficult to appreciate the severity of global warming because we can't easily see, touch, hear or smell it. Surely, if the planet is getting warmer and warmer then we should have noticed a bigger difference in temperature?

To understand global warming, we need to differentiate between the weather (the current conditions) and climate (the pattern of weather over a number of years). It's true that colder countries still experience cold winters but studies have recorded that the global average temperature has risen 33.8°F (0.99°C) from the mid-twentieth century to 2016, which itself became the sixteenth year since 2001 to become one of the seventeen warmest years on record.

Although global warming isn't tangible, its effects can be seen in how the weather and environment have changed over the years. The most significant and obvious change is to the polar ice caps, which have been melting at rates never seen before. For example, the US Glacier National Park has only 26 of 124 ice caps left and the ice sheet in Greenland loses approximately 300 gigatons (300 billion tons) of ice per year.

As a result of both the ice caps melting and the expansion of water as it warms, sea levels are rising. For example, from 2005 to 2015, the oceans' water levels rose by 1.3 inches. Again, this may not sound like a dramatic increase, but just this slight change means the atmosphere holding more warm moisture could make floods and storms more frequent and aggressive in susceptible areas.

An example of the real effect climate change is already having could be seen in 2017, when category-four hurricane Harvey hit the Texas coast in America and killed 14 people, while tens of thousands had to evacuate their homes. Shortly after this event, three more hurricanes (Irma, Jose, and Maria), which passed through the northeastern Caribbean, were recorded as category three or higher on the Saffir-Simpson hurricane wind scale, meaning they were all major hurricanes that caused devastating to catastrophic damage. Although hurricanes are common in this part of the world, especially between August and October, what has piqued researchers' interest is the number of major hurricanes recorded in such a short space of time over a small area. Many are concluding that this unusual pattern in serious weather events is a direct consequence of climate change.

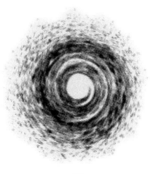

# THE EFFECT OF GLOBAL WARMING ON THE OCEANS

The greenhouse gases that are released into the atmosphere create a blanket between the sun and Earth so that the sun's heat gets trapped in the Earth's atmosphere; a large amount of this heat is absorbed by the ocean—almost 20 times more than by the atmosphere. Much like humans who cannot sustain a rise of 37.4°F above the average core body temperature of 98.6°F, the average ocean's temperature also needs to be strictly controled for its ecosystems to survive. However, since the mid-twentieth century, researchers have recognized a small rise (just 1.8–3.6°F) in the ocean's temperatures that they have linked to a variety of impacts, such as polar wildlife habitats being threatened, sea and shellfish having to relocate and becoming diseased, and a record number of coral reefs being recently affected by bleaching.

Bleaching occurs when algae is expelled from corals because the water is either too hot or too cold. Occasionally in recent years, there have been events where bleaching was a result of a drop in the sea water's temperature, but the majority of bleaching incidents around the world, especially at present, are due to overheating. When a coral reef is bleached, there is a chance of it recovering, but what we see more often now is a rise in cases of a whole coral reef dying because of repetitive overexposure to heat. The demise of a reef can be seen from its discolored appearance; after a while it will eventually completely erode to leave an empty void that was once inhabited by an entire ecosystem. While coral reefs only take up a small percentage of the ocean, they are home to a quarter of all marine life.

This is a global problem that needs to be addressed quickly if there is any hope of restoring the reefs to their normal condition. In 2005, approximately half of the Caribbean's reefs died. In 2016 and 2017, ARC Center of Excellence recorded a widespread bleaching event in the Great Barrier Reef that affected 900 miles of coral, leaving just the southernmost third untouched. Although there is a possibility that these corals might be able to survive events like this, there is a greater chance of additional bleaching if temperatures continue to stay the same or rise even more—this may sadly result in the corals' death.

To find out more, watch the compelling documentary *Chasing Coral* on Netflix.

## WHAT WILL HAPPEN WHEN WE USE ALL THE EARTH'S FOSSIL FUELS?

Many people worry that we won't have a good enough alternative to fossil fuels if we run out of them. However, the bigger issue we face is what the planet will look like after we have exhausted these energy sources. NASA has predicted that sea levels will rise by a minimum of 3 feet over the next century, while more extensive studies suggest that if we were to use up all of the Earth's remaining fossil fuels, sea levels could potentially rise by nearly 200 feet and flood most major cities. Additionally, temperatures will continue to rise and the weather will be more unpredictable. There will also be more frost-free seasons, which will affect a number of ecosystems as well as the agricultural industry.

## HAS OUR LOVE OF FOSSIL FUELS GONE TOO FAR?

Unfortunately, the damage caused by burning fossil fuels is irreversible. If we continue to use them as we have done over the past two centuries, the harm we would inflict on the planet would be catastrophic. However, more recently we have become increasingly conscious of the negative effects these energy sources have on our planet and it is apparent that our effort to start using greener, renewable energy sources is on the rise. For example, here is a snapshot of the UK's energy consumption in the past 20 years:

→ Since 1990, fuel use has decreased by 16.6 percent and energy consumption has fallen by the equivalent of 19.6 million tons of oil from 1990 to 2014.

→ Natural gas—the least damaging fossil fuel to the environment—has become the most used fuel since 1993, while coal use has decreased by 52.9 percent since 1990.

→ In 1990, 91.6 percent of energy consumed came from fossil fuels; in 2014, 85.2 percent of energy consumed came from these sources. While this still sounds high, 7.1 percent came from renewable and waste energy sources, which indicates that the UK is trying to introduce greener alternatives.

# WE DON'T HAVE TO SACRIFICE A STRONG ECONOMY FOR A HEALTHY ENVIRONMENT.

## DENNIS WEAVER

## WHAT ARE THE GREENER ALTERNATIVES TO FOSSIL FUELS?

→ **Nuclear energy**—this is generated by splitting atoms. Fossil fuels are still used in the process but considerably fewer of them, meaning lower costs and a huge fall in the release of greenhouse gas emissions. Nuclear energy currently only provides 6 percent of the world's energy, as there is a lot of controversy surrounding the process. The biggest risks include potentially fatal nuclear accidents (such as those in Chernobyl and Fukushima), management of removing nuclear waste safely, and nuclear power introducing more terrorist and military threats.

→ **Hydropower**—this type of energy is generated mainly from hydroelectric dams. It is clean, reliable, and efficient. In fact, hydropower turbines are capable of converting 90 percent of energy into electricity, as opposed to 50 percent of fossil fuels used in combustion (the process of burning something) being wasted in production. Building dams and hydroelectric power plants is expensive, but once they have been completed, maintenance costs are usually low. However, there are drawbacks; for example, the habitats of fish and wildlife are often destroyed during the construction of the dams and there is the possibility of drought—which will potentially be a more common occurrence with climate change. There may also not be enough suitable reservoirs to generate sufficient energy.

→ **Solar and wind power**—quite simply, these sources are derived from the sun and wind, respectively. Like hydropower, they are clean, reliable, and have created a wealth of jobs. Although the installation of solar panels is expensive, using solar energy is free and would probably offset the costs of using fossil fuels in the long run. Its main disadvantage is that if there is no sunlight, no energy is generated. This is especially problematic in winter months and in countries with high rainfall, although battery back-up systems are able to store the excess energy created. Similarly, wind is inconsistent and the installation of the turbines is expensive, plus complaints have been made about the noise and visual pollution from those who live nearby. Despite this, these sources of energy seem to be gaining more interest from governments and energy firms—in fact, in 2015 the first solar-powered plane, *Solar Impulse*, flew around the world without the aid of any fuel! Hopefully, this is just a glimpse of the future of renewable energy sources!

# *Industrial*
# AGRICULTURE

## WHAT IS INDUSTRIAL AGRICULTURE?

Also known as "intensive animal farming" or "factory farming," industrial agriculture refers to managing vast numbers of livestock and crops to meet the growing demands for meat and dairy produce. Farming has become more and more intensive due to the increase of the world's population, which was at 7.6 billion people as of September 2018. Unsurprisingly, to meet the demands of the consumer, mass farming poses many ethical and moral issues and has become a huge talking point in the media and among the public in recent years.

## HOW HAS FARMING CHANGED?

### PAST

→ Two hundred years ago, 90 percent of America's population produced its own food.

→ In 1940, each farmer produced enough food for 19 people.

→ Farm work would be done by hand or with horse-drawn carriages.

→ Animal and crop disease led to food shortages.

# PRESENT

→ Only 2 percent of the world's population produces food for everyone else.

→ With technology, each farmer is able to produce enough food to feed hundreds of people.

→ Machines such as tractors, combine harvesters, plows, and so on, make farming more efficient.

→ Biotechnology (the use of living organisms to perform industrial tasks) and genetic engineering (the modification of genes to produce better or new organisms) increase crop yield and animal breeding, helping to quicken the farming process and make it more reliable.

# NATURE PROVIDES A FREE LUNCH, BUT ONLY IF WE CONTROL OUR APPETITES.

WILLIAM RUCKELSHAUS

## SO HOW DOES PRESENT FARMING AFFECT THE ENVIRONMENT?

The way our predecessors farmed could be defined as what we now call "organic farming." Today, the "conventional" way of farming is usually in factories or large controlled areas of land and the produce is shipped globally. Although it may seem like the most efficient method, studies suggest that industrial agriculture struggles to feed the planet, destroys ecosystems on land as well as in the ocean, and is a huge contributor to global warming.

### HOW HARMFUL IS INDUSTRIAL AGRICULTURE? THE FACTS

→ One-third of global greenhouse emissions come from our worldwide food production.

→ In 2015, the UK produced 49.1 million carbon dioxide-equivalent tons of green-house gas emissions from agriculture, accounting for 10 percent of all greenhouse gases it generated that year and equivalent to emissions produced by using 10.1 million passenger vehicles for a year straight.

→ On average, America produces 1 kcal of food energy for every 3 kcal of fossil fuel emissions—this doesn't factor in the extra output of energy for processing and transporting the food.

→ The demand for agricultural land has destroyed over 260 million acres of forest in America and 3 million acres of rainforest in Brazil.

→ In 2013, 183 million tons of fertilizer nutrients were used, while it is estimated that this figure will rise to 200 million tons by 2018.

> → Each year, approximately 3 million tons of pesticides are used in agriculture.

## HOW DO CHEMICAL FERTILIZERS AND PESTICIDES HARM THE PLANET?

The three main chemical elements found in fertilizers are nitrogen, phosphorus, and potassium. These are used to help plant and crop growth, yet it is estimated that only 33 to 50 percent of fertilizers are absorbed by the plants. The rest is either absorbed by the soil—changing its acidity which can then impede plant diversification and growth— or is washed into streams, rivers, lakes, and eventually the sea. Once it finds its way into natural sources of water, the fertilizer increases the growth of algae, which in turn depletes the levels of oxygen in the water and forces fish and other marine wildlife to move elsewhere, or kills them. These areas of low oxygen are called "dead zones." In 2017, scientists recorded that the Gulf of Mexico's dead zone measured 8,776 square miles, while the average size of it over the previous five years was 6,700 square miles.

This is the result of nutrient pollution, primarily used in agriculture, running into the Mississippi River and flowing down to the gulf.

Pesticides comprise approximately 1,600 different chemicals. According to studies, only 0.1 percent of those used in agriculture successfully control the target pests; the other 99.9 percent impacts the environment, such as harming and killing birds and beneficial insects that ingest the chemicals while they eat crops, and increasing mutations in marine life via the pesticides being carried into natural sources of water.

## IMPACT OF PESTICIDES ON WILDLIFE

→ **Birds**—impacts vocals, meaning it is difficult for them to perform their mating calls and reproduce.

→ **Bees**—makes them drowsy, resulting in poor mobility and navigation and unusual feeding behaviors. Also affects their reproduction and development. Without bees, we would struggle to produce enough food (one-third of what we eat depends on their pollination), yet there has been a huge decline in the number of honeybee colonies since the late 1990s due to the pesticides we are using on crops. There is a glimmer of hope though for bee colonies in the UK and across Europe, as a total ban on bee-killing pesticides has been agreed. The US is petitioning to do the same.

→ **Amphibians**—there has been a growing number of frogs with mutations and deformities that are said to be linked with these chemicals.

→ **Whales, dolphins, and seals**—weakens their immune systems.

→ **Humans**—disrupts hormone messaging systems.

SOMEDAY WE SHALL LOOK BACK ON THIS DARK ERA OF AGRICULTURE AND SHAKE OUR HEADS. HOW COULD WE HAVE EVER BELIEVED THAT IT WAS A GOOD IDEA TO GROW OUR FOOD WITH POISONS?

JANE GOODALL

## INDUSTRIAL AGRICULTURE
## AND WATER—DAMAGE AND DEMAND

Irrigation (the application of controlled amounts of water to plants) is one of the main contributors to the detrimental effects food production is having on the environment. Worldwide, an estimated 70 percent of water use goes on agriculture (mainly irrigation), while the industrial and municipal sectors account for 30 percent combined. The demand for water for irrigation is starting to surpass the supply and many aquifers are drying up quicker than they can replenish themselves. And the facts speak for themselves: in America, an estimated 600 trillion gallons of water is used to produce the corn necessary to feed US cattle populations.

While irrigation is a short-term wonder for land that is too dry to produce good crop yields, it also damages soil after a length of time via waterlogging and inadvertent salinization (the process of increasing salt content). The Food and Agriculture Organization of the United Nations (FAO) has found that approximately 46 percent of the world's irrigated soil is affected by these two issues to some degree.

# INDUSTRIAL AGRICULTURE
# AND ENERGY—DAMAGE AND DEMAND

The food supply industry, from farm to supermarket, is one of the biggest users of fossil fuels, accounting for 20 percent of human-generated greenhouse gas emissions. Transport, processing, and packaging all contribute to this staggering figure. Studies estimate that the average American ready-meal travels approximately 1,500 miles before it ends up on a plate and, if fruit and vegetables aren't in season, or can't grow in a specific region of the world, they have been recorded to travel up to 2,300 miles to make sure they are available there.

Waste of food energy in large-scale meat production is another cause for concern. The conversion of grain into meat is energy-intensive and the input to output is greatly uneven. On average, it takes 15.5 pounds of grain to create 2 pounds of beef, 9 pounds of pork, and just over 4.5 pounds of chicken. In America, roughly 24 billion pounds of beef is produced every year, requiring 168 billion pounds of grain, 85 percent of which is wasted food energy.

# WE SHOULD ALL GROW OUR OWN FOOD AND DO OUR OWN WASTE PROCESSING, WE REALLY SHOULD.

## BILL GATES

# HOW DO FEEDLOTS HARM THE ENVIRONMENT?

Much of the livestock in the world is reared and fed in restricted and controlled areas of land, where production can be intensive. Today, "intensive farming" is a term most often used with regard to cattle reared for meat production and has surpassed "traditional" farming methods due to the sheer volume of livestock needed to feed us. As animals are separated from their natural habitat, their excrement, which was once beneficial to crop growth, is unsafely disposed of in bulk on patches of land that become environmental hazards. This waste releases harmful gases, such as methane, hydrogen sulphide, and ammonia, which contribute to serious respiratory and cardiovascular diseases and play a part in global warming. Excrement also finds its way into natural water sources and harms marine ecosystems.

# DEFORESTATION

## WHAT IS DEFORESTATION?

Deforestation is the removal of forests and rainforests by humans in order to use the land for non-forest purposes. The cut-down trees are used for building materials or are sold as fuel before the land is converted into farmland or developed for urban use. Although humans are the cause of the vast majority of deforestation the world over, natural occurrences such as wildfire and overgrazing also contribute to the demise of woodland and the stunted growth of young trees.

## SO HOW DOES DEFORESTATION AFFECT THE ENVIRONMENT?

The most obvious effect is the release of carbon dioxide into the atmosphere. The world's forests currently store approximately 280 billion tons of carbon dioxide, but with each tree that is cut down, a little more is pumped into the atmosphere, significantly adding to the rise in global warming. Crucially, trees also help absorb vast amounts of greenhouse gases from the Earth's atmosphere while transferring oxygen back into the air—without them, carbon dioxide levels would outweigh oxygen levels and life on Earth would no longer be able to sustain itself.

Another huge effect deforestation has on the environment is the removal of plant and animal habitats. Eighty percent of animals and plants rely on forests and rainforests for shelter and food. If they aren't killed in the process of deforestation, they are very unlikely to be able to adapt to their new surroundings when their habitats are wiped out.

Then there is the problem of eradicating trees from the planet's water cycle. Soil is constantly kept wet and full of nutrients due to the canopy that trees create in forests and rainforests. Without the protection of trees from the sun's glare, the soil would quickly dry out and turn the land into unfertile deserts.

# A NATION THAT DESTROYS ITS SOILS DESTROYS ITSELF. FORESTS ARE THE LUNGS OF OUR LAND, PURIFYING THE AIR AND GIVING FRESH STRENGTH TO OUR PEOPLE.

FRANKLIN D. ROOSEVELT

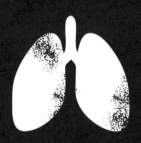

## HOW HARMFUL IS DEFORESTATION? THE FACTS

→ Each year deforestation accounts for the removal of trees from land equivalent to half the size of England.

→ Studies suggest that if we keep tearing down rainforests at the same rate we are at the moment, they could completely disappear within the next hundred years.

→ Removal of forests accounts for 12–17 percent of greenhouse gas emissions per year.

→ The Amazon rainforest contributes 20 percent of the world's oxygen.

→ Europe, America, and Japan use up to 70 percent of paper produced in the world and almost 50 percent of the world's timber.

- → Almost half of the world's tropical rainforests have been partly or fully removed, yet they provide the habitat for 6 to 7 percent of the planet's plant and animal species.
- → Thirteen species of trees in India were named as endangered and critically endangered between 2013 and 2017.

## HOW HAVE WE LET DEFORESTATION BECOME SUCH A GLOBAL PROBLEM?

In an overpopulated world, where the accumulation of material goods is at an all-time high and trading is most people's sole means of survival, it's not difficult to imagine how greed has got the better of us. The following list includes the main contributors of deforestation:

→ **Agricultural industry**—with a growing human population comes more demand for food and commodities. Sugarcane, soybean, and palm oil farming are the main culprits of agricultural deforestation as the cultivation of these crops requires the removal of trees while their production also harms the environment—for example, planting palm oil emits carbon dioxide as it degrades peat soils and burning sugarcane causes air pollution and impacts health.

→ **Ranching**—Brazil is one of the world's leading exporters of beef and has cleared an area the size of Italy from the Amazon rainforest. According to researchers, between 1993 and 2013 the number of cattle in the Amazon increased by 200 percent, reaching a total of nearly 60 million cows. As the demand for meat grows, this in turn affects the need for more crops for feeding and more land for the cattle to inhabit.

→ **Logging**—this is the act of chopping down trees for timber. As new regulations have been put in place to help the reduction and regrowth of forest areas, illegal logging is becoming more apparent. Studies show that up to 28 percent of the EU's timber exports could be unlawful.

→ **Infrastructure**—globalization has created a demand for new roads to be built, meaning huge areas of forest are wiped out for construction; this accounts for 10 percent of deforestation worldwide. Another 10 percent of the world's total contribution to deforestation is due to the extra urbanization that emerges from the construction of these new roads.

→ **Mining**—this accounts for 7 percent of deforestation in Asia, Africa, and Latin America. Areas of forest are often rich in minerals, such as gold, coltan, diamonds, uranium, manganese, and copper, and their extraction requires mass removal of trees.

➜ **Charcoal and wood for fuel**—across the tropics, especially in developing countries, approximately 1.4 billion cubic meters of firewood and 40 million tons of charcoal are used and produced respectively, per year.

IT IS UPSETTING THAT MANY PEOPLE DON'T SEEM TO OBSERVE WHAT'S HAPPENING TO THE ENVIRONMENT, WHAT'S HAPPENING IN TERMS OF GLOBAL WARMING, THE LOSS OF HABITATS AND WILD THINGS.

JOANNE WOODWARD

## HOW DOES PALM OIL IMPACT
## THE ENVIRONMENT AND WILDLIFE?

Palm oil is a cheap and versatile raw material, which is used in approximately 40 to 50 percent of household items, from cooking oil and cosmetics to cereals and soaps. This economic but un-environmentally friendly substance is one of the biggest causes of deforestation in Indonesia and Malaysia, where parts of rainforest equivalent to the size of 300 soccer fields are being cut down every hour.

While a vast range of wildlife is affected, the main endangered species is the orangutan. In Borneo and Sumatra, approximately 1,000 to 5,000 orangutans are killed each year and around 90 percent of their habitats have been destroyed in the past 20 years in order to meet the demand of palm oil production.

When palm oil is turned into a biofuel (a fuel derived immediately from living matter), the production also generates large quantities of smoke, as timber and forest undergrowth is burned to make way for the plantations: this leaves a carbon footprint five times larger than that of diesel.

# PALM OIL—THE HIDDEN INGREDIENT

A surprising number of common household items, such as lipstick, instant noodles, detergent, ice cream, cookies, and packaged bread contain palm oil. However, from assessing the ingredients list, it's often difficult to tell which items are made with palm oil, as the substance and its derivatives take a number of names. It is often found labeled as: vegetable oil, vegetable fat, palm kernel, palm kernel oil, palm fruit oil, palmate, palmitate, palm olein, glyceryl stearate, stearic acid, elaeis guineensis, palmitic acid, palm stearin, palmitoyl oxostearamide, palmitoyl tetrapeptide-3, sodium laureth sulfate, sodium lauryl sulfate, sodium kernelate, sodium palm kernelate, sodium lauroyl lactylate, hydrogenated palm glycerides, ethyl palmitate, octyl palmitate, or palmityl alcohol.

## MEDICINE AND DEFORESTATION

Each day, thousands of compounds from plants and animals are used to create medicines. The pharmaceutical industry in 2014 was worth more than 1 trillion American dollars and as many as 80 percent of people in certain countries rely on medication every day. There are 50,000 known medicinal plants in the world, 50 percent of which are primary ingredients in medications. However, due to deforestation, around one-fifth of these plants are at risk of extinction. Some of the most common endangered and threatened species due to pharmaceutical demand are:

→ **Tetu lakha (*Nothapodytes foetida*)**—this small tree is found in south Indian and Sri Lankan rainforests. It is predominantly used in anti-cancer drugs.

→ **Costus or kusta (*Saussurea lappa*)**—a saw-wort found in India. Its root is used in medication for chronic skin disorders.

→ **Yellow Himalayan Fritillary (*Fritillaria cirrhosa*)**— a tendrilled fritillary native to China, used to treat respiratory infections.

WE ARE DESTROYING
THE WORLD'S GREATEST
PHARMACY. IT IS VERY
IMPORTANT THAT WE
PROTECT THE RAINFOREST
IN EVERYTHING THAT WE DO.

CHRIS KILHAM

## HOW CAN WE MAKE MEDICINAL PRODUCTION SUSTAINABLE?

Of course, medicine is essential in all of our lives at some point and it would be a challenge to reduce production. The biggest problem, however, lies in how pharmaceutical companies source the natural compounds. According to research, an estimated two-thirds of the 50,000 medicinal plants used are harvested from the wild. In the UK, only 5 out of 16 herbal companies grow any of the medicinal plants they use as opposed to harvesting from the wild, and even then, it's only a small proportion.

Making this industry more sustainable means focusing on controlling harvesting programs more efficiently. Some plants, such as rosemary, thrive when they are harvested. Yet India's most popular medicinal plant, Ashwagandha (*Withania somnifera*), has seen a great decline, as it doesn't take well to harvesting, especially on such a commercial level. By focusing on ways to ensure the long-term availability of this and other endangered plants—for example, researching into alternatives and ways to use all of the plant instead of a small part, or harvesting and cultivating without degrading the natural environment—the medicinal industry and forests will become more sustainable.

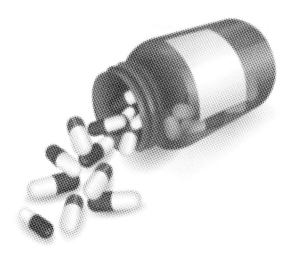

# HE THAT PLANTS TREES LOVES OTHERS BESIDE HIMSELF.

## THOMAS FULLER

## HOW ARE WE TRYING TO OFFSET DEFORESTATION?

→ The international body Sustainable Landscapes Partnership (SLP) is supporting 5,500 farmers to improve the quality and quantity of commercial commodities such as rubber, cocoa, and coffee worldwide.

→ Brazil reduced deforestation by 70 percent between 2004 and 2013 under the Amazon Regional Protected Areas (ARPA) program, which now protects nearly 173 million acres of the Amazon rainforest.

→ In China, residents must plant at least three trees in "the great green wall" (a man-made forest) every year—in 2009, 14.5 million acres of forest were created.

→ A number of governments, businesses, and civil society organizations signed the New York Declaration on Forests (NYDF) in 2014. The program proposes many future goals and aims, including:

- ➔ At least halve the rate of natural forest loss by 2020 and end it by 2030.
- ➔ Restore forest and cropland areas equivalent to the size of India.
- ➔ Eliminate deforestation from certain agricultural production commodities, such as palm oil, soybean, paper, and beef products, by 2020.
- ➔ If all the targets of the incentive are achieved, carbon emissions could be reduced by 4.5 billion to 8.8 billion tons per year by 2030.

# *Human*
# POPULATION

## THE PROBLEM WITH HUMANS

We invented plastics; we realized fossil fuels could be burned to create energy; we went from hunting for our food to having it farmed; and we found ways to transform natural resources into commodities. We dominate the world in numbers and intelligence, making it suffer slowly in our greed, but will these two factors mean the demise of our species and the eventual destruction of the planet?

## A RISING POPULATION

There's no supply without demand, and unfortunately the need for energy, food, water, and raw materials is increasing at an alarming rate due to the steep increase of the world's population. The human race began 200,000 years ago. By 10,000 years ago, the human population had grown to 1 million, then by the year 1800 there were 1 billion of us. This figure grew to 3 billion by 1960 and then, in the handful of decades since, has more than doubled to over 7 billion humans occupying the planet as of 2017. And it doesn't stop there: studies estimate that by 2050 the human population will increase to a staggering 9 billion.

# WHEN THE LAST TREE IS CUT DOWN, THE LAST FISH EATEN AND THE LAST STREAM POISONED, YOU WILL REALIZE THAT YOU CANNOT EAT MONEY.

CREE INDIAN PROVERB

## HOW ARE HUMANS DAMAGING THE PLANET? THE FACTS

→ The way we live is a primary contributor to climate change—since 1998, ten of the warmest years since data collection began have been recorded.

→ Excessive water wastage is apparent everywhere—for every burger produced, 3,000 liters of water are used; 1 cup of coffee (before water has been added) takes 100 liters to make; to fill a 1-liter bottle of water, around 3 liters of water are wasted.

→ Urbanization is wiping out nature—19 cities in Brazil have doubled in size over the past decade (ten of which are in the Amazon) and by 2050, an estimated 70 percent of us will be living in existing or new cities.

→ Household energy consumption generates 60 percent of global greenhouse emissions and 50 to 80 percent of total land, material, and water use.

# BUT MAN IS A PART OF NATURE, AND HIS WAR AGAINST NATURE IS INEVITABLY A WAR AGAINST HIMSELF.

RACHEL CARSON

## HUMANS AND CONSUMERISM

Instead of nurturing nature, we are destroying it. Just for fashion, animals are abused and slaughtered; for our vanity, they are tested on; for snapping an awesome social media profile picture, they are cruelly handled; for trying an odd delicacy, they are killed for a tiny part of their bodies. Here are some of the most common animals that are on the endangered species list due to our obsession with consumerism:

→ The population of the Hawksbill turtle has declined by an estimated 80 percent over the past century. It is mostly killed for its shell and meat.

→ Approximately 73 million sharks are killed each year to make the so-called "luxury fare" shark fin soup, where 98 percent of the shark is wasted. Once they have cut off the fin, the fishermen throw its body back into the ocean, letting it sink to the bottom.

→ The largest living mammal on earth, the blue whale, may soon cease to exist. Overall, it is estimated that 200,000 blue whales were killed in the first half of the twentieth century; only 3,000 to 5,000 are left on the planet.

→ Commercial fishing has added many species to the endangered list, including the Hawaiian monk seal, Fraser's dolphin, and the Vaquita porpoise. In America, around 1.9 billion pounds of seafood is wasted each year.

→ Over 75 million animals are killed for their fur, annually. (Additionally, creating a fur garment takes 20 times the energy needed to produce an item with fake fur.)

→ From 2007 to 2014, the number of rhinos poached in South Africa increased by 9,000 percent, while 1,054 rhinos were killed in South Africa in 2016 alone.

## IS THERE A SOLUTION?

There are too many of us living on the planet: fact. The logical yet unrealistic solution would be to limit the number of children people are having. But, morally and ethically, this is a step too far—it is in our genetic coding to reproduce—plus the issues that would arise from imposing this regulation would most likely actually speed up the process of the destruction of humankind through war and hate.

The only other way to limit the damage to the planet from mass consumerism is to cut out or reduce consumption. Do you really need an upgrade to the latest phone, or can you cope with your current model that's working perfectly well? Do you need to turn on the central heating just so you don't have to wear a sweater? Is it necessary to buy new clothes when you've already got a wardrobe full, half of which still have the tags attached to them? We are all guilty of desiring what we don't have—society has made us that way—but if every individual changed their lifestyle to become more environmentally friendly, the impact it could have on the planet might be hugely positive.

# THE GREATEST THREAT TO OUR PLANET IS THE BELIEF THAT SOMEONE ELSE WILL SAVE IT.

ROBERT SWAN

# HOW CAN WE REDUCE OUR CARBON FOOTPRINT?

# BUSINESSES

## REDUCING PLASTIC WASTE

→ Assess packaging. Marks and Spencer has recently redesigned and repackaged more than 140 products to minimize plastic waste, helping cut 75 tons of it every year.

→ Offer free tap water to the public if the business is public-facing; this will reduce the quantity of plastic bottles bought in shops.

→ Try consolidating orders so items are bought in bulk to reduce packaging and fuel emissions.

→ Have team-building days that contribute to plastic clean-up in your local area.

→ Use recycled toner cartridges and send empty ones back for recycling.

→ Phase out physical magazines and bulletins and circulate them electronically instead.

→ Buy second-hand furniture and equipment. Donate furniture and equipment that's no longer in use to a re-use charity.

→ Use drinking glasses and mugs instead of plastic cups.

- → Provide staff with a food preparation area and cooking/storage facilities, such as a microwave and fridge, to encourage them to bring food from home in reusable containers.
- → Re-use packaging that is shipped to you.
- → Invest in high-quality, longer-lasting equipment.

# THE ULTIMATE TEST OF MAN'S CONSCIENCE MAY BE HIS WILLINGNESS TO SACRIFICE SOMETHING TODAY FOR FUTURE GENERATIONS WHOSE WORDS OF THANKS WILL NOT BE HEARD.

GAYLORD NELSON

## REDUCING COMPANIES' CARBON FOOTPRINTS

→ Purchase economy-class tickets instead of first- or business-class, especially if it's for a short-haul flight. Flying first-class leaves a carbon footprint roughly nine times the size of economy's.

→ Attend virtual meetings instead of traveling long distances.

→ Set up bicycle rack facilities to encourage staff to bike their commute.

→ Use responsible and local suppliers and manufacturers.

→ Integrate a car-sharing scheme into your company (http://business.liftshare.com/products/car-sharing).

→ Switch to high-efficiency energy and have regular audits on your cooling and heating systems.

→ Install motion sensors to efficiently manage electricity use.

→ Encourage your team to turn off computers and switch off electrical devices, including coffee pots, microwaves, and so on, at the end of the day.

- → Set computers to energy-saving mode.
- → Increase the number of work-from-home days per month to reduce the company's carbon emissions.
- → Purchase a program or software to measure energy and cost savings.
- → Change your thermostat settings out of hours.
- → Propose meat-free Mondays (www.meatlessmonday.com).
- → Start a monthly collection to buy local fruit in bulk.
- → Invite a Greenpeace Greenspeaker to give a presentation on environmental issues (www.greenpeace.org.usa).

# KEEP CLOSE TO NATURE'S HEART... AND BREAK CLEAR AWAY, ONCE IN AWHILE, AND CLIMB A MOUNTAIN OR SPEND A WEEK IN THE WOODS. WASH YOUR SPIRIT CLEAN.

JOHN MUIR

## PREVENTING DEFORESTATION

→ Offset paper waste by donating money to plant trees; Sainsbury's has planted 2.2 million trees since 2004.

→ Experiment with going paper-free for a week.

→ Make double-sided printing the default setting.

→ If printing a document, use wider margins, single spaces between lines, and a smaller font.

→ Unsubscribe from unwanted junk mail, newspapers, and magazines.

→ Shred unwanted paper and use as packaging material.

→ Place a recycling box next to every printer.

→ Buy only chlorine-free paper.

→ Provide hand towels or air dryers in the bathrooms instead of paper towels.

→ Avoid buying single-use packets of creamer and sugar.

→ Buy an acre of rainforest to help create permanently protected nature reserves (www.worldlandtrust.org/projects/buy-acre).

# INDIVIDUALS

# REDUCING PLASTIC WASTE

→ Stop using plastic drinking straws.

→ Buy a reusable flask to fill with water from the tap; if you have to-go coffee frequently, keep a reusable mug on you.

→ Chew mints instead of gum.

→ Make a conscious effort to buy items that come in cardboard boxes, as they are easier to recycle.

→ Buy food in bulk and store it in containers.

→ Create homemade cleaning products and re-use the bottles once empty; lots of ideas can be found on the internet.

→ Use a razor with replaceable blades.

→ Buy cotton swabs with paper stems and never flush plastic ones down the toilet.

→ Always taketote bags out with you if you're going shopping.

→ Avoid using face washes and toothpaste with "polypropylene" or "polyethylene" in the ingredients list.

→ Pack your lunch in reusable containers.

→ Buy loose fruit and fresh bread to cut out the waste of plastic packaging.

→ Use bars of soap instead of liquid handwash.

→ Buy second-hand furniture and equipment and donate items you don't use to re-use charities.

THE ONLY WAY FORWARD, IF WE ARE GOING TO IMPROVE THE QUALITY OF THE ENVIRONMENT, IS TO GET EVERYBODY INVOLVED.

RICHARD ROGERS

## REDUCING YOUR CARBON FOOTPRINT

→ Choose to buy from brick-and-mortar stores rather than online.

→ Carpool.

→ Walk or bike rather than drive short distances and, where possible, use public transportation for longer trips.

→ Buy local and organic produce and attend food markets.

→ Check labels on food and clothes to know where they are made/sourced from.

→ Eat less meat, especially red meat; studies suggest vegans have a carbon footprint of 20 percent less than a meat-eating person.

→ Make your home better insulated.

→ Replace inefficient old gas or oil boilers.

→ Hang your clothes out to dry rather than use a tumble dryer.

→ Buy less—only purchase items you need.

→ Switch off devices and plugs when not in use instead of putting them on standby.

→ Look into using more renewable energy sources, such as solar panels.

THE EARTH WE ABUSE AND
THE LIVING THINGS WE
KILL WILL, IN THE END,
TAKE THEIR REVENGE;
FOR IN EXPLOITING
THEIR PRESENCE WE ARE
DIMINISHING OUR FUTURE.

MARYA MANNES

## PREVENTING DEFORESTATION

→ Donate, volunteer, fundraise or campaign for an environmental charity.

→ Buy wood and timber products that have the Forest Stewardship Council (FSC) label.

→ Recycle and buy recycled products.

→ Switch to paperless billing.

→ Adopt a tree (www.worldlandtrust.org/projects/plant-tree).

→ Cut back on or remove meat from your diet: many forests are cut down to make space for livestock.

→ Avoid products that contain palm oil without the RSPO or Green Palm label, as they have not been made with certified sustainable palm oil. Visit www.ethicalconsumer.org/shoppingethically/palmoil-freelist.aspx for a list of products that are free of/use the least palm oil.

→ Keep electronic devices for longer—especially mobile phones—and buy new products made from recycled materials.

# A HEALTHY ECOLOGY IS THE BASIS FOR A HEALTHY ECONOMY.

CLAUDINE SCHNEIDER

# RESOURCES

All websites accessed 30 November 2017.

## INTRODUCTION
→ www.theguardian.com/environment/2011/mar/02/when-discover-climate-change

→ www.theguardian.com/environment/2005/jun/30/climatechange.climatechangeenvironment2

→ www.ecology.com/2010/09/15/secret-world-energy

## PLASTICS
→ http://news.bbc.co.uk/1/hi/magazine/7516859.stm

→ www.cutplasticsheeting.co.uk/blog/2015/02/09/21-facts-about-recycling-plastics

→ www.bbc.co.uk/news/science-environment-40654915

→ www.alternet.org/environment/its-time-stop-using-plastic-drinking-straws-theyre-bad-environment-and-harm-wildlife

→ www.theguardian.com/environment/2017/jun/30/tackling-the-plastic-bottle-crisis-and-our-wider-disregard-for-nature

- www.biologicaldiversity.org/campaigns/ocean_plastics
- www.telegraph.co.uk/science/2017/05/18/prince-wales-plastic-worlds-oceans-growing-human-disaster
- www.explainthatstuff.com/bioplastics.html
- www.lifewithoutplastic.com/store
- www.cleanwater.org
- www.nurdlehunt.org.uk/whats-the-solution/global-response.html
- https://oceanservice.noaa.gov/news/sep15/icc.html
- www.thelondoneconomic.com/food-drink/pub-chain-bans-straws-attempt-become-environmentally-friendly/19/04
- www.theguardian.com/environment/2016/jul/30/england-plastic-bag-usage-drops-85-per-cent-since-5p-charged-introduced
- www.theguardian.com/lifeandstyle/2017/jun/23/tattooing-avocados-helps-keep-up-supply-of-smash-hit

- → https://uk.lush.com/article/our-environmental-policy
- → www.theguardian.com/sustainable-business/2017/jul/30/retailers-manufacturers-reduce-plastic-use-waste-lily-cole-ellen-macarthur
- → www.telegraph.co.uk/science/2017/02/13/johnson-johnson-ditch-plastic-cotton-buds-save-oceans
- → http://nordic.businessinsider.com/sweden-is-so-good-at-recycling-its-now-getting-a-deposit-refund-system-for-plastic-bags-2017-5

## FOSSIL FUELS

- → www.ons.gov.uk/economy/environmentalaccounts/bulletins/ukenvironmental accounts/2016#fuel-use
- → www.desmog.uk/2017/07/31/citizens-paying-fossil-fuel-subsidies-taxes-and-their-health-report
- → https://ourworldindata.org/how-long-before-we-run-out-of-fossil-fuels
- → www.popsci.com/burning-all-fossil-fuels-could-raise-sea-levels-by-200-feet#page-2

→ www.livestrong.com/article/126194-disadvantages-fossil-fuel

→ https://nuclear-energy.net/advantages-and-disadvantages-of-nuclear-energy.html

→ https://naturalresources.house.gov/issues/issue/?IssueID=8267

→ http://energyinformative.org/hydroelectric-energy-pros-and-cons

→ www.solarimpulse.com

→ www.conserve-energy-future.com/disadvantages_solarenergy.php

→ www.conserve-energy-future.com/pros-and-cons-of-wind-energy.php

→ www.ucsusa.org/global_warming/science_and_impacts/science/cold-snow-climate-change.html#.WeoL0GhSyUk

→ www.independent.co.uk/environment/glaciers-melting-earth-crust-shape-change-climate-change-global-warming-nasa-solitary-wave-rink-a7762756.html

- www.nasa.gov/feature/goddard/warming-seas-and-melting-ice-sheets
- www.theguardian.com/environment/2017/aug/29/how-did-climate-change-worsen-hurricane-harvey
- www.nytimes.com/2017/09/19/us/hurricanes-irma-harvey-maria.html
- www.bitsofscience.org/climate-change-chasing-coral-movie-watch-7376
- https://oceanservice.noaa.gov/facts/coral_bleach.html
- www.coralcoe.org.au/media-releases/two-thirds-of-great-barrier-reef-hit-by-back-to-back-mass-coral-bleaching
- www.chasingcoral.com

## INDUSTRIAL AGRICULTURE

- www.earthisland.org/journal/index.php/elist/eListRead/organic_farming_vs_industrial_ag_time_to_change_the_debate
- www.epa.gov/energy/greenhouse-gas-equivalencies-calculator

- www.gov.uk/government/uploads/system/uploads/attachment_data/file/666073/agriclimate-8edition-8dec17.pdf
- www.fao.org/3/a-i4324e.pdf
- www.onegreenplanet.org/animalsandnature/factory-farming-is-killing-the-environment
- www.newsweek.com/nutrient-pollution-hurts-fish-study-says-340983
- www.noaa.gov/media-release/gulf-of-mexico-dead-zone-is-largest-ever-measured
- wwf.panda.org/what_we_do/footprint/agriculture/impacts/pollution
- http://sos-bees.org
- www.ncbi.nlm.nih.gov/pmc/articles/PMC1240832/pdf/ehp0110-000445.pdf
- www.wsj.com/articles/is-feedlot-beef-bad-for-the-environment-1436757037
- https://ourworld.unu.edu/en/the-shame-of-concentrated-animal-feedlots

## DEFORESTATION

→ www.conserve-energy-future.com/various-deforestation-facts.php

→ www.nationalgeographic.com/environment/global-warming/deforestation

→ www.sciencemag.org/news/2015/05/brazil-cattle-industry-begins-help-fight-deforestation

→ http://edepot.wur.nl/297258

→ www.allianz.com/en/about_us/open-knowledge/topics/environment/articles/150329-the-top-ten-drivers-of-deforestation.html/#!m31a773ce-2877-49ee-8c38-b056eba77d6c

→ www.ucsusa.org/sites/default/files/legacy/assets/documents/global_warming/UCS_Driversof Deforestation_Chap8_Woodfuel.pdf

→ www.saynotopalmoil.com/Whats_the_issue.php

→ www.worldwildlife.org/pages/which-everyday-products-contain-palm-oil

→ www.worldbank.org/en/news/feature/2015/01/13/la-deforestacion-un-dolor-de-cabeza-para-la-medicina-natural

→ www.newscientist.com/article/dn4538-herbal-medicine-boom-threatens-plants/#.VLaVBNLF81L

→ www.statista.com/topics/1764/global-pharmaceutical-industry

→ www.theguardian.com/world/2004/jan/07/environment.health

→ www.worldbank.org/en/results/2013/10/09/Brazil-protects-Amazon-increasing-size-protected-areas

→ www.conservation.org/projects/Pages/sustainable-landscapes-partnership-northern-sumatra-indonesia.aspx

→ www.un.org/climatechange/summit/wp-content/uploads/sites/2/2014/07/New-York-Declaration-on-Forest-%E2%80%93-Action-Statement-and-Action-Plan.pdf

→ http://sciencing.com/things-being-done-deforestation-6080.html

## HUMAN POPULATION

→ www.theguardian.com/environment/2013/jun/30/
   stephen-emmott-ten-billion

→ www.forbes.com/sites/energysource/2012/08/13/
   microsofts-stephen-emmott-sounds-alarm-on-
   population-surge-in-theatrical-lecture/#56b038
   4b5ba6

→ www.grist.org/living/consumerism-plays-a-huge-role-
   in-climate-change

→ www.marineinsight.com/environment/10-
   endangered-ocean-species-and-marine-animals

→ http://wwf.panda.org/what_we_do/endangered_
   species/cetaceans/about/blue_whale

→ www.wildaid.org/sharks

→ www.huffingtonpost.com/ted-danson/wasted-catch-
   its-time-to_b_5006453.html

→ www.cryoftheinnocent.com/facts

→ www.savetherhino.org/rhino_info/poaching_
   statistics

## HOW CAN WE REDUCE PLASTIC WASTAGE? BUSINESSES

→ www.theguardian.com/sustainable-business/2017/jul/30/retailers-manufacturers-reduce-plastic-use-waste-lily-coleellen-macarthur

→ www.theguardian.com/sustainable-business/2017/aug/29/business-plastic-packaging-waste-solutionsenvironment-slimbox-splosh-borough-market-marksspencer-lush

→ www.frn.org.uk

→ www.rethinkrecycling.com

## HOW CAN WE REDUCE OUR CARBON FOOTPRINT? BUSINESSES

→ http://documents.worldbank.org/curated/en/141851468168853188/pdf/WPS6471.pdf

→ http://acre.com/news/blog/2014/07/7-ways-businesses-could-reduce-their-carbon-emissions

## HOW CAN WE PREVENT DEFORESTATION?
## BUSINESSES

➜ www.greatbusinessdebate.co.uk/text_fact/8-ways-business-is-helping-to-protect-the-environment

➜ https://trees.org

➜ www.greeneducationfoundation.org/national greenweeksub/waste-reduction-tips/tips-for-the-office.html

➜ www.sciencealert.com/working-green-50-tips-to-reduce-your-offices-waste

## HOW CAN WE REDUCE PLASTIC WASTAGE?
## INDIVIDUALS

➜ www.greeneducationfoundation.org/national greenweeksub/waste-reduction-tips/tips-to-use-less-plastic.html

➜ www.hgtv.com/design/decorating/clean-and-organize/9-homemade-cleaning-products

➜ https://myplasticfreelife.com/plasticfreeguide

## HOW CAN WE REDUCE OUR CARBON FOOTPRINT?
### INDIVIDUALS

➜ www.theguardian.com/environment/2017/jan/19/
how-to-reduce-carbon-footprint

## HOW CAN WE PREVENT DEFORESTATION?
### INDIVIDUALS

➜ www.scientificamerican.com/article/how-to-help-
prevent-cutting-down-the-amazon

➜ www.ethicalconsumer.org/shoppingethically/
palmoilfreelist.aspx

➜ www.mnn.com/family/family-activities/blogs/5-ways-
to-stop-deforestation

## IMAGE CREDITS